KU-778-908

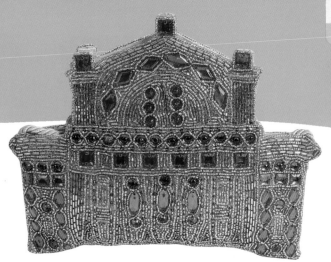

Contents

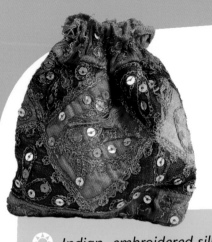

Indian, embroidered silk-and-sequin drawstring bag

Recycled juice-pack belt bag from the Philippines

Small fabric bee pouch from China

Money containers

All over the world people design and create money containers – such as bags, purses, pouches, wallets and beltbags – in many different shapes, sizes and colours.

They may be made from beads, leather, plastic, wood, metal, paper, felt, woven camel hair, recycled juice packs and even bottle caps.

Laminated cotton swimming bag from England

Finely woven wool shoulder bag from Bolivia

World of Design

Anne Civardi

Photography by Sam Hare & Jane Paszkiewicz

W
FRANKLIN WATTS
LONDON•SYDNEY

First published in 2007 by Franklin Watts
338 Euston Road, London NW1 3BH

This edition 2011.

Franklin Watts Australia
Level 17/207 Kent Street
Sydney NSW 2000

Design: Rachel Hamdi and Holly Fulbrook
Editor: Ruth Thomson

The author would like to thank these people for the loan of items from their collection:
Shikasuki Vintage Boutique, Primrose Hill, London NW1 8LD (www.shikasuki.com):
vintage metal butterfly bag, 4; vintage PVC vinyl poodle bag, 5; vintage wooden
box bag, 5; vintage beaded fish purse,10. Steinberg and Tolkien: vintage box
bag, 2; vintage jewelled palace bag, 3; vintage box bag, 22. Doy Bags
(www.doybags.com): foil belt bag, 3; foil purse, 11; foil MP3 player holder, 15.
Joss Graham (www.jossgrahamgallery@btopenworld.com): silk and sequin
bag, 4; embroidered fob watch cover, 4; woven wool purse, 5;
embroidered amulet holder, 11; embroidered fabric wallet, 18.
Tyrrell Katz (www.beachfactory.com): laminated cotton bags and
towels, 4, 8. Zip••it ™ (www.zipitstyle.com): zip bag, 11.
Islington Education Library Service (www.objectlessons.org):
sequin and mirror bag, 2, 14; Indian drawstring bag, 3; Afgan
bag, 14; Victorian belt bag, 19; newspaper bags, 23. With
special thanks to Diana Marsh for her help and advice.

A CIP catalogue record for this book is available
from the British Library. Dewey Classification: 746.9

ISBN 978 1 4451 0159 0

Printed and bound in China

Franklin Watts is a division of Hachette
Children's Books, an Hachette Livre UK company.
www.hachette.co.uk

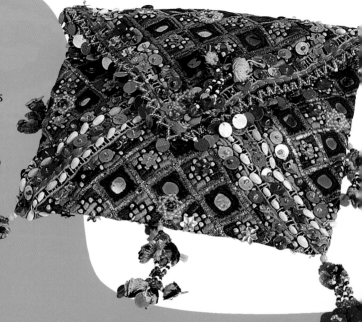

✺ *Vintage, American PVC vinyl bag with appliqué poodle of cut glass stones and beads*

✺ *Bead and cowrie shell bag made in Kenya*

This book shows you bags and purses in all kinds of different styles, and various clasps and fastenings used to close them.

It will help you to understand how people design and create money containers. It will show you a few simple sewing stitches so that you can make some bags and purses of your own.

✺ *Embroidered fob-watch cover purse from Afghanistan*

✺ *Vintage, hand-painted, wooden box bag from Japan*

✺ *Hand-tooled leather wallet from Morocco*

✺ *Vintage, metal and stone butterfly bag from America*

Drawstring bags

These bags are called drawstring bags because they open and close by pulling, or drawing, a cord, string or strap tight.

☼ Cotton and plastic were laminated (bonded or pressed) together to create the fabric for this English swimming bag. The laminated cotton makes the bag waterproof.

☼ Made in a Guatemalan village, this colourful cotton fabric backpack was hand-woven on a treadle (foot) loom. Mayans have been weaving stripy designs like this for more than 500 years.

Look closer

- The towel was designed to match the football motifs on the bag.

- There is a handy pocket on one side which closes with a zip.

- The two drawstring shoulder straps allow the bag to be used as a backpack.

Look closer

- This bag is made of hand-embroidered fabric.
- It is decorated with strings of glass beads.
- Tassels of colourful cotton thread are attached to the ends of the beads.

✹ This beaded and finely embroidered drawstring bag was made by a Pashtun woman living in the mountains of Afghanistan.

Look closer

- The drawstring strap of this bag is held tight with a small leather strip.
- The diamond pattern was created with thin strips of white leather.
- There are several pockets around the bottom of the bag.

✹ This Moroccan bag is made of cow hide. The hide was treated in a huge vat of pink dye and pigeon droppings.

✹ The little fish of this fabric Chinese purse is for coins. The big one is for notes. In China, fish are a symbol of good luck.

Making a drawstring bag

1 Cut out a paper pattern (template) 40cm x 94cm. Pin it to the fabric and cut around it.

- 0.5m cotton-backed plastic fabric
- paper • scissors
- pins and a needle • thread
- a big safety pin • 1m cord

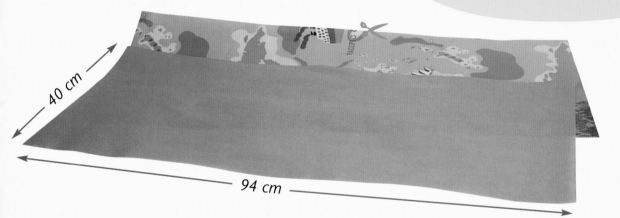

40 cm

94 cm

2 With the shiny side facing down, fold over and pin 4cm at either end.

4 cm

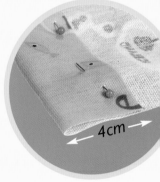

4 cm

4cm

3 Using running stitch (see page 30), sew along both folds, 1cm from the edges. Remove the pins as you go.

4 Fold the fabric in half with the shiny sides together. Sew the sides together, 1cm from the edge, until you reach the folded ends.

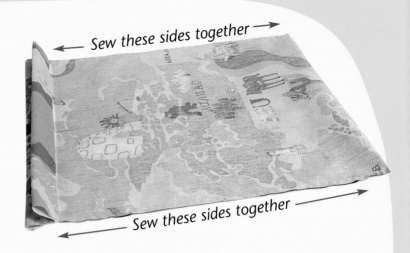

Sew these sides together →

← *Sew these sides together*

← *Sew these sides together* →

5 Turn the bag, so that the shiny side faces out. Knot both ends of the cord. Poke a big safety pin through one knot. Thread the pin through the gap in the folded ends of the bag.

Thread the safety pin and cord through the gap.

6 Once the cord is threaded through, take off the safety pin and knot the ends together. Pull the cord to gather the top of your swimming bag tight.

Knot the ends of the cord together.

9

Purses and pouches

Purses and pouches are small so they can fit into a handbag or pocket. They are used to carry coins and have fastenings which stop the coins from falling out.

Created in a village high up in the Himalayan mountains of Nepal, this felt purse, or pencil case, was hand-made from sheep's wool. Nepalese people also use felt to make rugs.

Look closer

- The pouch is made from a square of fabric.
- It is embroidered with a geometric pattern.
- Pushing the glass bead up or down the cords opens or closes the pouch.

This pouch was made by the Banjara tribe in India. It was used to hold an amulet. An amulet is thought to bring good luck and give protection.

- This purse is beaded on both sides in the shape of a stripy fish with a tail, mouth, eyes and fins.

- The lines of beads are designed to look like tiny fish scales.

Women in the Philippines make bags and purses from recycled foil juice packs. They weave strips of foil together to create a colourful pattern.

Created in Korea about 40 years ago, this beaded purse has a clasp made of two metal balls that snap together.

Look closer

- The bag below starts out as a long flat zip made from two different colours.

- When it is completely zipped up, it forms a bag with a handle.

This zip bag was designed in America and won the Product of the Year award at a show in Boston. The biggest Zipit bag is made with a zip that is more than 690cm long.

Making a perfect pouch

1 Cut a paper template, 12cm x 12cm. Fold the fabric in half and pin the template on top.

paper template

12cm

12cm

2 Cut around the template, so you have two pieces of fabric, exactly the same size.

Use double thread. Sew about 1cm from the edge.

3 With the fabric the right way up, use backstitch (see page 30) to sew the two squares together, about 1cm from the edges.

Tip: The fabric will only fray up to where you have backstitched.

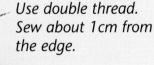

4 Make five bead and sequin tassels, each about 8cm long.

5 As you finish each tassel, sew it on to the fabric square, as shown.

Tip: Make sure you sew the bead tassels inside the line of backstitching.

6 Cut four lengths of cord, each 25cm long. Knot one end of each piece.

7 Poke a small hole in each corner of the fabric square, just inside the line of backstitching. Push a length of cord through each hole. Thread the four lengths of cord through the big bead and knot the ends together.

Tip: Push the bead down to close your pouch. You could use it to hold a good luck charm.

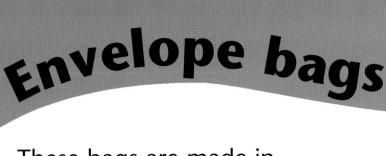

Envelope bags

These bags are made in the style of an envelope with a flap that opens and closes.

Both these bags have loop fastenings. The one on the embroidered Afghan bag above loops over a tassel. The one on the Moroccan silk bag loops over a crocheted silk button.

Look closer

- The embroidered bag below is decorated with sequins, tiny mirrors and glass beads to make it sparkle.

- A diamond pattern has been created with gold thread.

- There are lines of small white shells sewn on the bag.

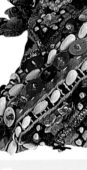

This antique bag from Pakistan was created from a large square of finely hand-embroidered and decorated cloth.

Created in England, this purse is made from cow-hide that has been dyed bright pink.

- The big turquoise leather button is a special design feature of this pink purse.
- The turquoise stitching matches the button and contrasts well with the pink cow-hide.

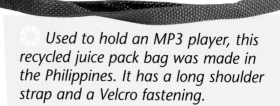

- The jewellery roll below has been edged with silk piping.
- It has two zipped pockets to hold jewellery.
- The rolled-up bag can be tied together with silk ribbons.

Used to hold an MP3 player, this recycled juice pack bag was made in the Philippines. It has a long shoulder strap and a Velcro fastening.

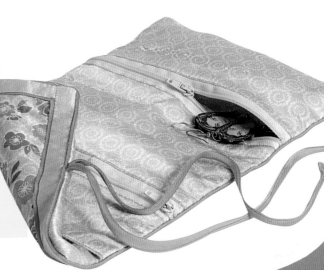

Used especially for holding small pieces of jewellery, this English jewellery roll is made from printed silk.

Making a wallet belt-bag

← 12cm →

← 12cm →

18cm

27cm

1 Using a paper template, 18cm x 12cm, cut a rectangle of felt. With another template, 27cm x 12cm, cut a rectangle of fake leather.

Leave open.

2 Glue the felt on to the fake leather close to the edges. Leave the top edge open to make a felt pocket for money notes.

← Glue these edges together. →

Glu the toge

← Glue these edges together. →

Overstitch edges together.

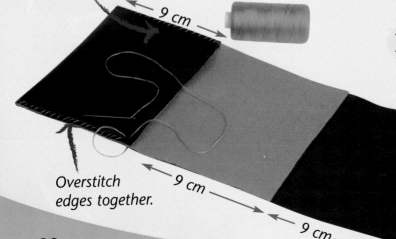

← 9 cm →

3 Fold up the felt end of the rectangle about 9cm. Overstitch (see page 30) the folded sides together to make a pocket for coins.

Overstitch edges together.

← 9 cm →

← 9 cm →

20

4 Fold the wallet in three, as shown. Glue three leather and felt squares as decoration to the top flap.

5 Cut two 6cm strips of self-adhesive Velcro, one hook side and one loop side. Stick them in place, as shown. Press them together to fasten the wallet.

self-adhesive Velcro

6 Glue a strip of fake leather, 5cm x 8cm to the back of the wallet as the loop for your belt.

belt loop

Tip: You can use the wallet by itself or as a belt-bag.

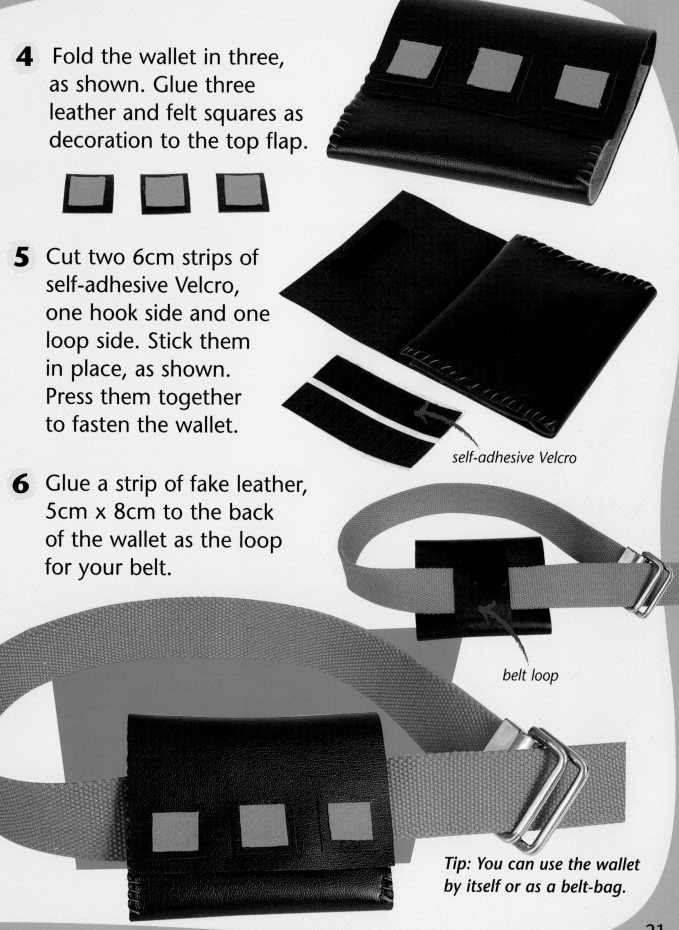

Recycled bags

In many parts of the world people recycle materials, such as boxes, fabric scraps, newspaper, bottle tops and even old records, to turn into useful bags.

This bag was made in Kenya from recycled bottle caps attached to a wire frame. The handles are made of coiled wire.

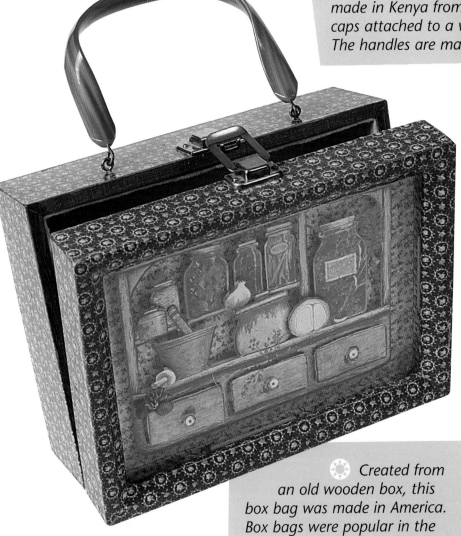

Created from an old wooden box, this box bag was made in America. Box bags were popular in the 1960s and 1970s.

Look closer

- Paper jars stand on a kitchen shelf inside the plastic window on the lid of this box bag.

- The bag has a hinged lid, a plastic handle and a metal clasp.

- A pattern of paper circles and flowers covers the outside of the box.

☀ *A group of women in South Africa earn a living by making rag bags like this from old t-shirts.*

Look closer

- The bag is made by pushing and knotting strips of old t-shirts through holes in hessian cloth.
- Because the knots of fabric look like kernels of corn, the group of women who make them are called 'Mielie', which means 'corn' in Swahili.

☀ *In India, newpapers are recycled into bags like these. The money raised from selling them helps pay for street children in Delhi to go to school, instead of pulling rickshaws or polishing shoes.*

☀ *Two old records have been included in the design of this funky plastic and metal American handbag.*

23

Making a disco-box bag

1 Take the label off the plastic box. Ask an adult to poke a hole into each end of the lid, as shown.

- an empty plastic box
- scissors ● wrapping paper
- acrylic paint and a paintbrush
- plastic jewels, scraps of lace, lengths of sequins and ribbon
- glue ● 0.5m cord

2 Cover the lid with two layers of acrylic paint. Leave it to dry.

3 Cut a strip of wrapping paper big enough to fit around the box. Glue it on.

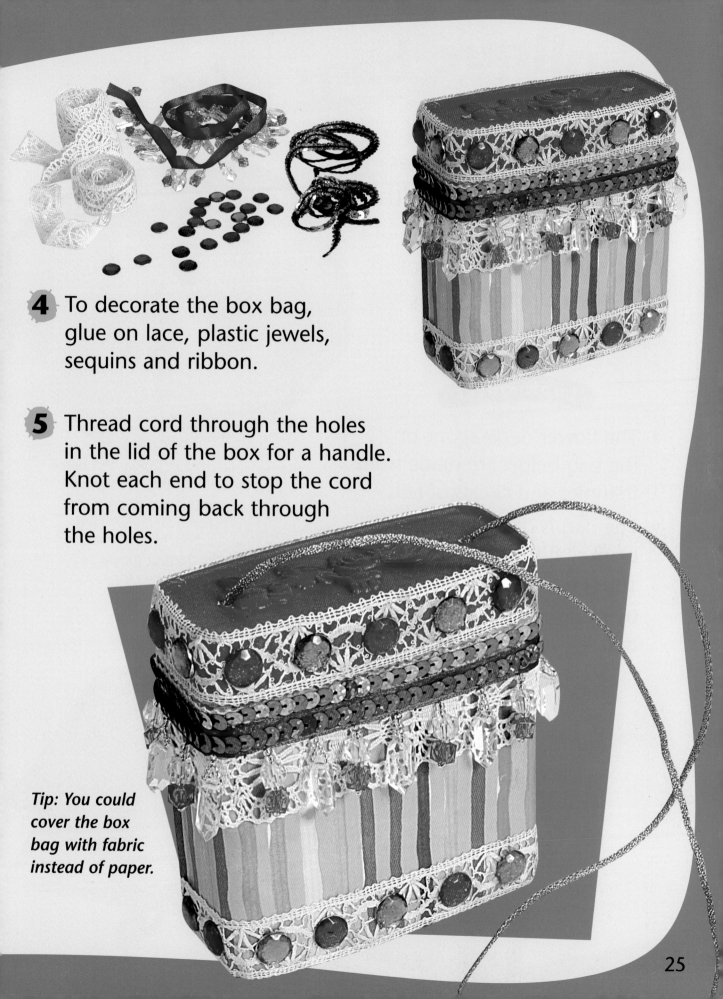

4 To decorate the box bag, glue on lace, plastic jewels, sequins and ribbon.

5 Thread cord through the holes in the lid of the box for a handle. Knot each end to stop the cord from coming back through the holes.

Tip: You could cover the box bag with fabric instead of paper.

Appliqué bags

All these bags and purses have been decorated with separate pieces of material sewn or glued on top of them. This technique is called appliqué.

Look closer

- The flower decorations on the bag below are made from triangles and circles of felt.
- The bag is decorated with blanket stitch (see page 30).
- The bow was created by plaiting three thin felt strips.

Created in China, this purse is made from pink and green plastic with a metal clasp that snaps shut. The high-heeled shoe was machine-stitched on to the front of the purse.

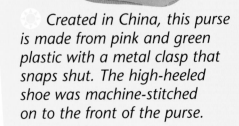

A sturdy metal popper closes this felt English envelope bag.

- This bag is appliquéd with pieces of old embroidered Indian fabric.

- A wide strip of fabric has been sewn on to look like a belt. Both pockets are edged with thinner strips.

- The bag is lined with a bright pink cotton fabric.

An old pair of blue jeans were used to design this crafty bag from America.

Look closer

- A dog's face with ears, eyes, a black nose and red tongue is appliquéd on to the bag below.

- It is sewn on with blanket stitch (see page 30).

This shoulder bag from England is made of felt. Felt is created from sheep's wool and other animal fibres. These fibres turn into a fabric when they are rubbed together in warm, soapy water.

Making an appliqué bag

1 Using a paper template, 36cm x 24cm, cut out two different coloured felt rectangles.

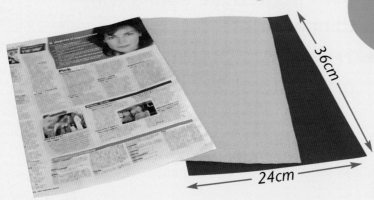

36cm

24cm

Use double thread to blanket stitch around edges.

2 Pin one felt rectangle on top of the other. Sew them together with blanket stitch (see page 30).

3 Fold up 12cm of one end of the felt rectangle to form a pocket. Glue or sew the edges together, as shown.

Glue or sew edges together.

24cm

12cm

12cm

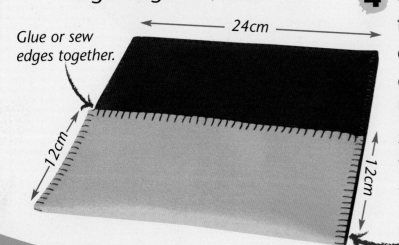

4 Using a paper template the size of a mug base, cut two felt circles. Use a smaller template to cut two more felt circles.

Glue or sew edges together.

5 Cut each felt circle in half and in half again, so you have 4 quarters. Cut each quarter in half to make 8 triangles of felt from each circle.

6 Glue the triangles of felt on to the bag to look like flowers. Glue felt circles on to the middle of each flower.

Tip: You can use as many or as few felt triangles as you like to form the flowers.

7 Sew two lengths of ribbon on to the bag, as shown. Tie them together to fasten the bag.

Tip: It is best to use fabric that doesn't fray when you appliqué.

Handy hints

You need to learn these simple stitches to make the projects in this book. To start, thread a needle and knot one end of the thread.

Running stitch

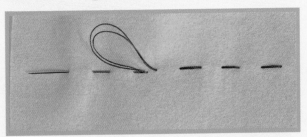

Make small stitches by pushing a threaded needle in and out of the fabric. Keep the stitches and spaces as even as possible. Finish off by sewing a couple of stitches on top of each other.

Backstitch

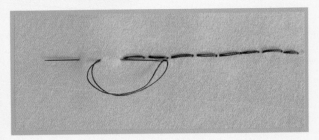

Make a stitch and a space through the fabric. Take the needle back over the space and bring it out the same distance in front of the thread. Repeat this, ending with two backstitches on top of each other.

Overstitch

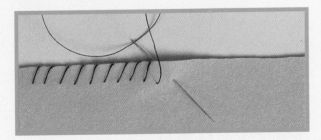

Make diagonal stitches over the raw edge of the fabric. Try to space them equally and make them all the same length. Be careful not to pull the stitches too tight. This stitch helps to stop fabric from fraying.

Blanket stitch

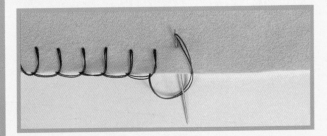

Close to the edge, push the needle from the front of the fabric to the back, with the point of the needle coming out in front of the loop made by the thread. Pull the needle and thread through until the blanket stitch is flat against the fabric.

Bags and purses are designed with all sorts of different clasps and fastenings. Look through the book to find which of these fastenings are used on which bag or purse.

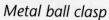

Metal ball clasp

Zip

Velcro

Plastic belt clasp

Bead and cord

Drawstring

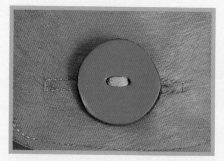

Button and button hole

Metal rings

Suitcase clasp

Loop over button

Metal popper

Ribbon

Glossary

amulet a charm worn on the body thought to have a magic power to protect against harm or injury

crochet needlework in which loops of thread or yarn are woven together using a hooked needle

embroider to create a design on fabric with needlework

lining the fabric used to cover the inside of something, such as a bag, purse or dress

motif a figure or shape that is repeated in a design

template a pattern, in this case made of paper, that is used to make an exact copy of an object or shape

Index